June

Dear Jen,

"If you can make it in New York
You can make it anywhere".

Our very best to you,

love,
Sy & Doryl Bekoff

NEW

This edition published in 1984 by
Bison Books Corp.
17 Sherwood Place
Greenwich, CT 06830

ISBN 0 86124 189 4

Printed in Hong Kong

The authors gratefully acknowledge
the help of Gianna Manferto and
Carlo De Fabianis

to Diana

YORK

PHOTOGRAPHY   MARCELLO BERTINETTI
ANGELA WHITE BERTINETTI

TEXT   MARCELLO BERTINETTI
ANGELA WHITE BERTINETTI
VALERIA MANFERTO DE FABIANIS

DESIGN   MARCELLO BERTINETTI

Bison Books

Preface

It's difficult for me to say why, or how, or even when the idea of New York first took root in me. Looking back on my encounters with that dramatic city, I feel a special fondness for that day in September 1981. Angela and I had just reached New York City in our camper. Weary from our journey but excited by our first glimpses of the city, we felt our hopes quickly dissolve into dismay as the frenzy and noise of New York engulfed us. New York was much more complicated than we had anticipated.

Where would we go? What would we do? Surrounded by so many options, all clamoring for attention, it was impossible to decide. We suddenly felt the need to be closer together, to recover the human dimension that the city, with its frenetic pace and its skyscrapers, seemed to have forgotten. We began to walk. Like children, we were fascinated, curious, enthusiastic and anxious.

The jostling crowds, the yellowness of the taxis, the procession of images we passed, the sun's reflection on the skyscrapers—all these things magically initiated us into a world very different from our own. There must be a special reason for us being here, I kept thinking, but what was it? And why New York?

It is true that only someone who has been in New York can imagine the terrific contradiction the city embodies. I felt that I could hate New York just as easily as I could love it, but no one feeling stayed long enough to claim center stage. I was captivated by the city's extraordinary charm, but I was repelled and mystified by its coldness and anonymity.

When I thought about New York after my return to Italy, a series of images would come to mind: peaks of skyscrapers jutting into torrents of rain or reflecting the red light of sunset, nights illuminated by neon signs, people swarming up and down avenues during rush hour, somber Rolls Royces gliding amidst the elegance of Park Avenue, serene skyline views from New Jersey and Brooklyn.

But there were other, nagging images: vagrants rummaging

through garbage cans, the dark and frightening atmosphere of 42nd Street, the giddiness of people in Central Park on Sundays. These things are just as much a part of New York, and as I contemplated them a complete picture began to form until I suddenly realized that New York had become very dear to me. And it was in such a state during a peaceful evening at home that I had the disturbing feeling that I had left something behind. It was an irresistible call. I had to go back.

The impressions of New York that haunted me were fixed only in my mind; my lens had missed them. The urge grew stronger to take the images that had become part of me, to seek them out again, and to fix them on film. I knew them by heart, and had begun to think about how to photograph them. And so, in May of 1982, we went back to New York.

It was with foolish self-assurance that we approached New York, then delved into it, by taxi. My certainty grew as we approached the center of the city. I went over in my mind the carefully arranged, detailed plans. Nothing, this time, would be left to chance. I would transform my feelings into pictures; I would capture New York.

The taxi slowed down and finally stopped, leaving us on the Avenue of the Americas. It took only a few moments of peering up at the towering buildings and watching people and cars pass by with giddy speed before my convictions collapsed. Once again I, with my meager intentions, was dwarfed by the imposing greatness of this city. And once again, I felt the city slipping away without my being able to grasp its intimate reality.

But time and chance allowed my to re-encounter the images which had filled my winter evenings: the evening light among the rooftops bordering Central Park, the sun glimmering between the colossal buildings of Sixth Avenue, the magnificient golden reflection of the twin towers of the World Trade Center at sunset, and then . . . the people: these New Yorkers who are so temperamental, so indifferent, and so strange.

I got to work, focussing my mind and my camera, allowing the city itself to dictate my photographs. When I left I finally felt satisfied, my anxiety dispelled. I couldn't repress a quiet smile while taking a farewell look at the 'Big Apple.'

Now, in the stillness of a country town, I sit in my quiet home among thousands of pictures and think of New York. I remember the narrow spaces in which the helicopters fly and the avenues with their thousands of synchronized traffic lights like some choreographed dance. Again, I feel that I have felt something behind, but this time it is different. The uneasiness is mixed with some measure of fulfillment.

Like every big city, New York has something elusive about it: the lives of all the people that populate it. New York lives off their joys, their sorrows, and their everyday doings, enriching itself with these vital impulses. Man, the single individual, can't understand and possess the gigantic soul of New York. Perhaps he can only guess it, perhaps for only an instant.

Marcello Bertinetti

THE BIG APPLE

When a person arrives in New York City for the first time he walks along with his eyes fixed on the imposing tops of the skyscrapers, neglecting everything else happening around him on the road. The variety of architectural styles and the sheer height of the buildings make a striking spectacle, especially if one thinks that the nucleus of this metropolis was only a little fortress in 1600, built by a Dutchman on a piece of land traded by the Indians.

Since that time, New York has swelled to enormous proportions, like a huge organism that compels its hosts to a hectic pace, defying them to retain an identity amidst the barrage of images. And yet, in a crazy and impassioned way, New Yorkers love their city. They couldn't live in any other town.

The size and vitality of New York is reflected in its vast transportation network. Intense traffic moves along its almost 6000-mile long road network. It's enough to think that it's served by no less that 120,000 taxis! Every day about four million people use the underground and, on the surface, another two and a half million crowd the buses.

New York seem bigger, higher and livelier than anywhere else. Pages and pages wouldn't be enough to describe it. In short, New York is New York!

17 *'The Big Apple' of New York, shown here on the lighted billboard below an advertisement for the Broadway musical,* **Barnum.**

19 *Third Avenue streamlines midtown Manhattan in the suffused light of dusk.*

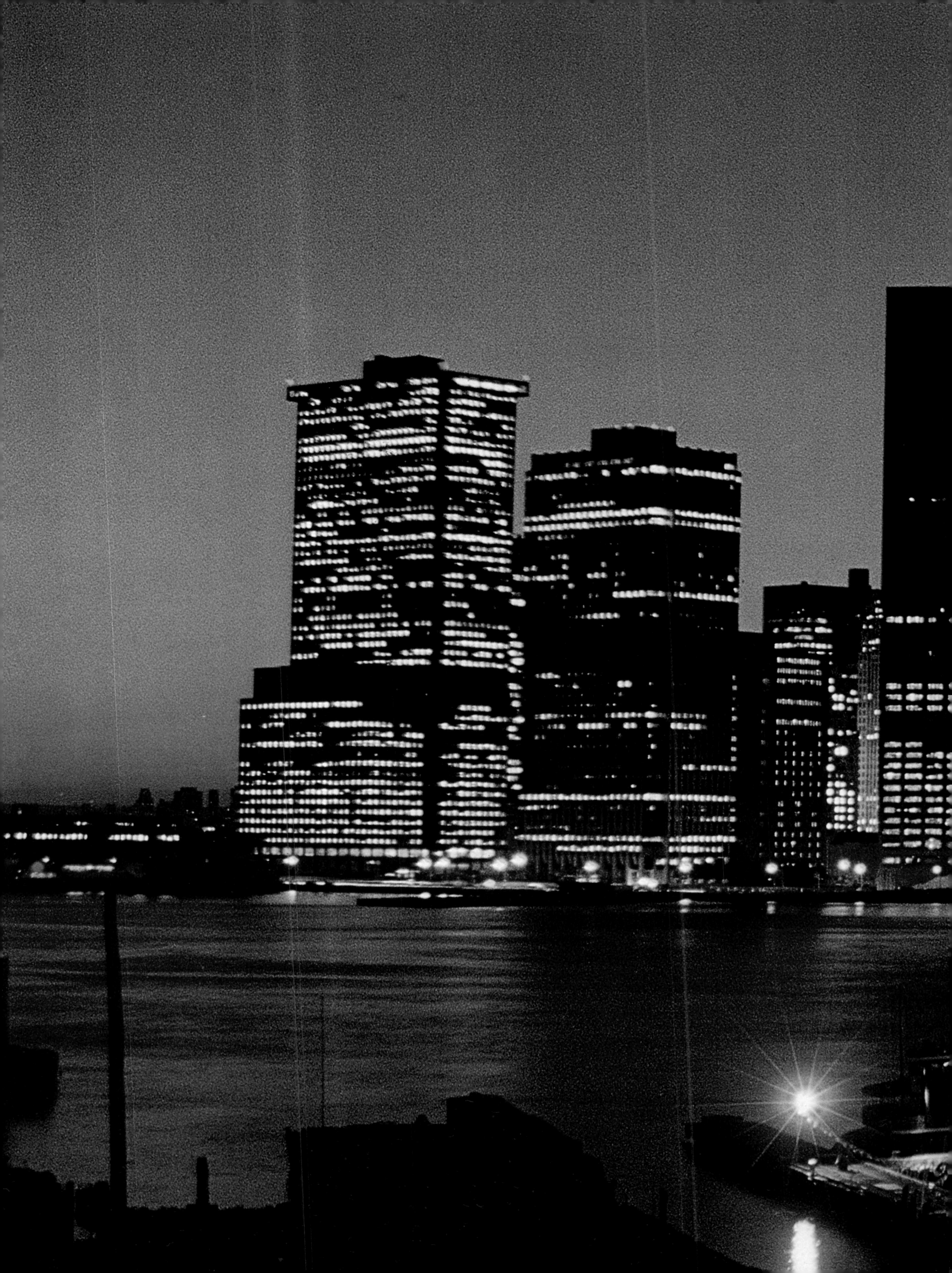

20–22 A rare and particularly charming New York sunset. The skyscrapers of the World Trade Center dominate the skyline.

23 A helicopter flying low over the Hudson River nearly skims the sails of a little boat. The Hudson, East and Harlem Rivers encircle Manhattan Island and flow into the Atlantic Ocean.

24/25 A view of midtown Manhattan from the panoramic terrace of the Empire State Building. Stylish Fifth Avenue runs down the center of Manhattan, dividing it into East and West.

26/27 An aerial view of Brooklyn and Manhattan Bridges. The Brooklyn Bridge was completed in 1883; it was the longest bridge existant at that time.

28. Sunday is a day of amusement and rest
in New York. Here, New Yorkers enjoy the
sun and the newspaper on the Promenade
in Brooklyn.

29 An aerial view of the southern tip of
Manhattan Island, encircled by the Hudson
and the East Rivers.

STREETS AND AVENUES

There is something deceptive but at the same time appropriate about Manhattan's road system—the center and soul of the city. Simple and functional, the streets and avenues are arranged in a grid. Viewed from above, they appear like a close-knit net broken up by blocks of gray buildings and streams of multi-colored traffic. The streets of the southern and oldest part of Manhattan and the diagonal Broadway defy this orderly scheme, winding randomly about.

Swooping down closer to, then into, the city itself, the feeling of orderliness vanishes. Crowds of people animate the streets and avenues, creating a captivating and varied spectacle. Every ethnic group, race, age and occupation seems well-represented on these streets; every mode of transportation flourishes—from skateboards to bicycles, from limousines to motorcycles, from trucks to taxis. And in this constant procession of people and vehicles, it is not unusual to see little carriages pulled by tired horses, indifferent to the chaotic traffic.

All this, together with the deafening noise and the gaudy colors, combine to give a particular atmosphere to the streets of New York. A certain adriotness and practice is necessary to be able to move calmly in the middle of it all. And still, pleasant surprises await in the little, almost provincial world along the side streets.

Heedless to the muted echo of traffic, an old man on a bench reads the newspaper and relishes the tepid warmth of the sun. Further along the street a group of boys plays baseball, while someone else meanders lazily along the sidewalk. Such extreme contrasts in such a narrow space may seem startling at first, but they are typical of New York.

31 The brightly lit town is always an extraordinary sight. The Avenue of the Americas is among the main arteries of New York. Radio City Music Hall can be seen on the right.

33 The traffic on Sixth Avenue is dense but flows quite rapidly because of the synchronized traffic lights and the regular street pattern.

34/35 Fifth Avenue sidewalks are usually crowded, especially at lunch time.

36/37 Fifth Avenue is one of the busiest avenues in Manhattan. Until the beginning of the twentieth century the city's rich middle classes lived here.

38 In September Little Italy becomes colorful and lively to celebrate St. Gennaro's Day with feasts, street fairs and parades. The procession goes along Mulberry and Grand Streets.

39 Park Avenue is the only avenue in Manhattan that has traffic flowing both north and south. The bright color of the taxis give it a festive appearance.

40 On Sunday morning the avenues of New York are quite uninhabited, so that a horse-carriage can stop undisturbed in the middle of the road.

41 On working days the city traffic swells enormously. A horse carriage travels with difficulty through a maze of cars.

42 A colorful mural on the wall of a building in Greenwich Village.

43 The intricate crown of the Helmsley Building in the foreground contrasts the modern monolith of the Colgate Palmolive Building on the right.

PEOPLE

There isn't one sphere of human life that doesn't find its biggest expression in New York. From Wall Street to the United Nations building to Madison Square Garden, New York seems to be the center of influence in nearly every area imaginable: theatre, sports, media, economics, politics. And indeed the people reflect this consciousness. In the squares and parks and along the streets, the faces of New Yorkers convey a feeling of their city's importance and their pride to be part of it.

Just as readily, though, a New Yorker will cite New York's exorbitant crime rate, enumerating suicide, delinquency and drug addiction statistics. They will talk about the crowds, the danger, the filth, the racial and ethnic tension, the homeless. The problems of New York appear insurmountable, and so New Yorkers have learned to live with them—to sidestep the danger, to negotiate the mean streets with feigned aloofness and indifference. Yet they are just as apt as any tourist to stop and gape at street scenes: a music show in Central Park, a young fire-eater on the sidewalk, teenagers on roller-skates weaving hand-in-hand through traffic. And why would anyone put up with New York's idiosyncracies if they did not love the place? They are as crazy as the city itself; they live in the heart of the world.

45 Roller-skates are one of the commonest means of transportation among young people, particularly in Central Park.

47 Light penetrates the cross-streets with difficulty, producing strange contrasts.

48/49 While a girl sunbathes on the roof of her house, life rolls by quietly and peacefully on the streets below.

50/51 A relaxing moment during lunch break.

52/53 Side-by-side with great wealth is the harsh reality of the tramps, who rummage through trash-cans in a daily struggle to survive.

54/55 Impromptu shows surprise and de-light at Lincoln Center. Here the two performers represent a colorful butterfly and an ethereal moth.

56 The old and young alike enjoy relaxing in
Central Park.

57 A pedestrian dares the traffic on a busy
avenue.

58 In Washington Square a young man amazes onlookers with a display of fire-eating.

59 A steaming manhole cover creates a hazy background for the colorful pedestrian.

60 People enjoy mingling and lingering in the city squares.

61 This foreshortening of 42nd Street can be compared to Montmartre, the artists' quarter of Paris.

62a St. Anthony and St. Gennaro are both commemorated in Little Italy each year.

62b Absorbed in an article, a New Yorker uses a magnifying glass to read **The Daily News.**

62c A policeman is involved in an improvised show along the streets of New York.

62d Fixed chess-boards in a square in Washington Park attract crowds of chess-players.

63 Park Avenue is a study in haves and have-nots. Here, a lone vagrant searches for a treasure in the trash barrel while pedestrians swarm past.

a

b

c

d

GLIMPSES

Besides the bustling activity and the bona fide tourist attractions, New York offers glimpses, to the careful observer, of hidden corners and secret beauty. The composition of the city itself hints at a complex image that contrasts sharply with the monotony of other modern metropolises. For the astute visitor who can manage not to be overcome by the vast, clamorous, colorful and absorbing madness, New York harbors more private manifestations of its soul—the secret city of New York.

A steaming manhole cover, a creaking horse-drawn carriage, a colorful clothesline in the Bowery, a bohemian corner in Greenwich Village, a skyscraper's spire, the plethora of architectural styles—all these things characterize the unmistakable city in a suitably dynamic and elusive way.

65 Rockefeller Center is a cluster of twenty-one buildings located between Fifth and Seventh Avenues. A symbol of the power and wealth of New York, it is crossed by the private Rockefeller Plaza, which is closed one day every year.

67 The majestic Statue of Liberty was given to the United States by France to commemorate their alliance during the Revolutionary War.

68/69 An impressive steel structure in the New York port on the Hudson River. This type of structure was fashionable in the 1930s.

70/71 The enormous and ever-changing crowds of New York take on an ethereal quality in contrast to the stolid edifices of office buildings.

72 An unusual view of New York in the
Bowery, one of the poorest and most dan-
gerous quarters of the city. In the nineteenth
century it enjoyed a splendid period as the
center of the city's night life. It rapidly
declined until it reached its present sad
level.

73 Grand Central Terminal can be considered a little town within the town. From
it a vast network of subways and trains
emanates through the city, the boroughs
and the suburbs.

74 This stoop in Greenwich Village has a distinctively European look. This section of the city is considered to be the artists' quarter and relives the bohemian atmosphere of Saint Germain des Prés.

75 The horse-carriages, like any other public means of transportation, are equipped with regular number plates.

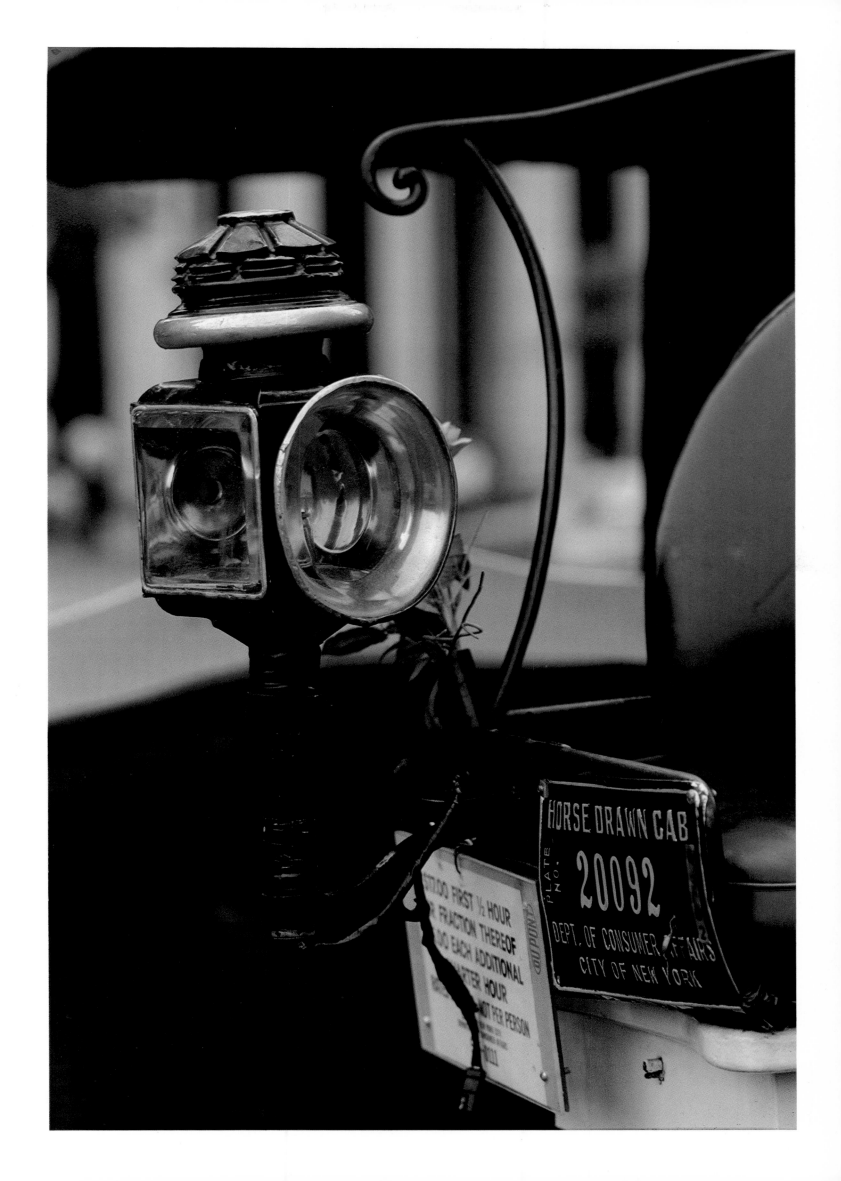

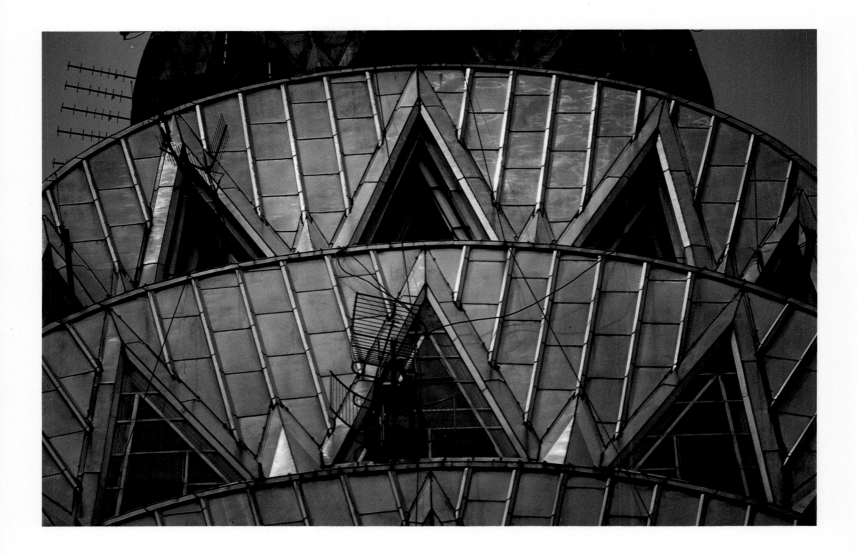

76 *The Chrysler Building on 42nd Street can be considered a homage to the car. It's an outstanding example of the Art Deco style of architecture.*

77 Manhattan is the only borough of New York City that uses steam to power the buildings' air conditioning and heating systems. Here, a cloud forms as hot and cool air converge.

MIRRORS

It is possible to say that New York leads a double life—one that is real and one that is reflected. In a city known for glitter and glamor, why would it be surprising that the buildings collect the glow of sunset in a magnificent play of lights?

And yet it is both awe-inspiring and thought-provoking that New York emulates itself in Manhattan Bay, in passing shop windows, in wet asphalt. The vanity and the quiet reflection, the grandeur and the illusion of New York are embodied in its mirrors.

The twin towers of the World Trade Center attract the golden reflections of sunset like magnificent monoliths rising from the earth. And if they are covered with gold, it is silver that covers the Citycorp Center when it juts unmistakably into the skyline.

The city fragments itself into intricate geometric designs and shimmering distortions. New York admires itself and seeks admiration from those who are seeing it for the first time and from those complacent people who have known and loved it for a long time.

79 *The rippling reflection of the twin towers of the World Trade Center in the Hudson River.*

81 *Windows of the Playboy Club on 59th Street distort the reflection of the Plaza Hotel.*

82/83 The reflection of low buildings super-
imposed on this colorful window display in
Greenwich Village creates an eerie effect.

84/85 Behind reflective windows, diners
relax in this haven from the hectic streets.

86 Reflected in a puddle, colors meld and
soften to create a pleasant effect.

87 The distinctive outline of the Citicorp
Center is reflected in a building on Lexing-
ton Avenue. The mass of the Citicorp Center
is supported exclusively by four enormous
pillars.

88 The Greenwich Savings Bank on East 57th Street is fragmented in a grid-like reflection.

89 A curved building facade creates a fun-house effect of the city traffic.

90 The rain gives a particularly bright and fascinating look to New York at night.

91 The camera distorts this reflective sky-scraper on 57th Street.

SKYSCRAPERS

The skyscrapers of New York are like cities unto themselves. Some, like the World Trade Center, have their own subway system and shopping center. Apart from their rich variety and their magnificence, the skyscrapers represent the seats of the largest multinational companies in the world and cultural, political and economic centers of primary importance.

Inside them decisions of world significance are made, the destinies of thousands of people are influenced, impossible dreams come true or are shattered, fortunes are made and great financial empires are destroyed.

Sometimes referred to as cold monsters of crystal and steel, these skyscrapers actually quiver with life and emotions. En masse, people stream in and out of them each day, creating a myriad of colonies, each with its own task.

The delightfully unique spire of the Chrysler Building, the 'cathedral in the sky' called the Empire State Building, and the mysterious hulks of the World Trade Center shrouded in fog comprise a skyline that speaks of history, of aspiration, of the immortality of man's endeavors.

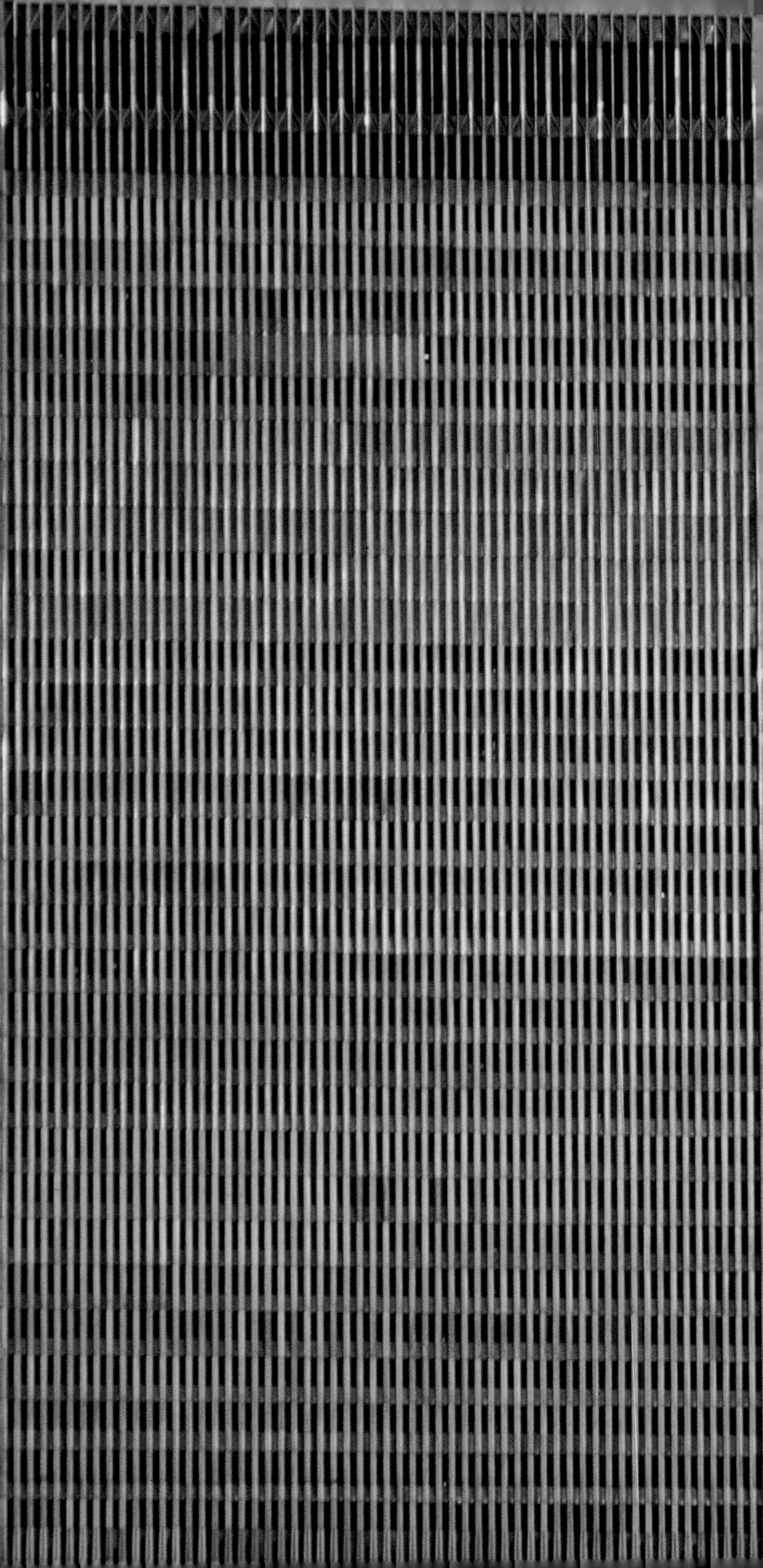

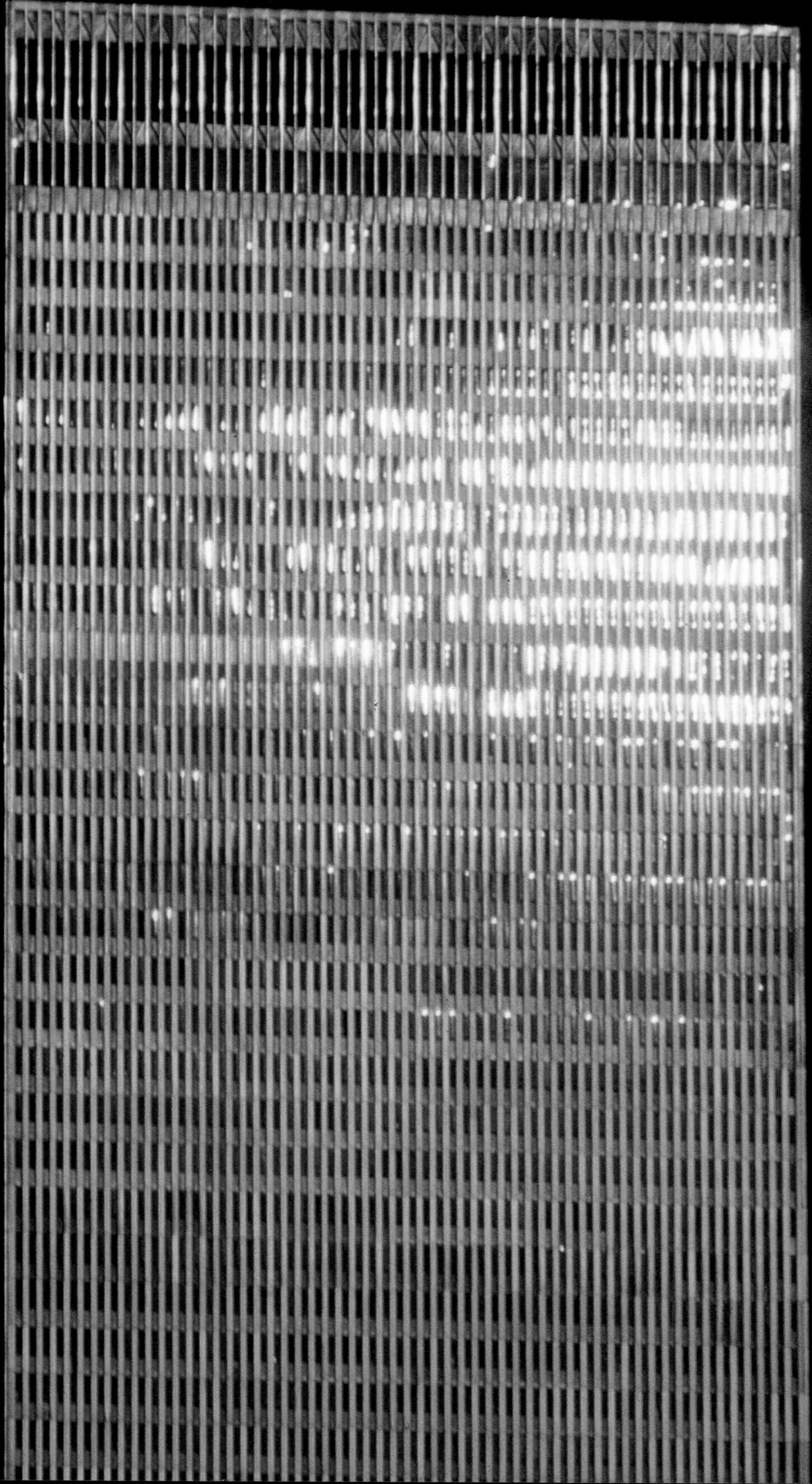

LIGHTS

If in every other town of the world rain creates a sad and gloomy atmosphere, in New York it has the opposite effect. Shiny pavement at night highlights and exalts the city's brightness and vitality. The lights double themselves in the puddles and refract themselves in the splashes which rise from the pavement as cars pass.

Lights characterize Manhattan at every moment of the day. A tender blue colors the city at dawn and suggests the reawakening of life. As the minutes pass it begins to permeate the streets, enter the houses, and turn out the lights of the street-lamps and shop windows. Then the streets fill up with people and noises, returning to their daytime rhythm.

At dusk, a rare sunset may fill the sky with red, multiplying in the mirrors of the skyscrapers and illuminating the faces of the people. The shadows of skycrapers lengthen as night comes suddenly, and New York switches on its multi-colored lights. Silhouettes of people linger before the fountain at Rockefeller Center and scurry through the lights of Times Square as headlights stream past. New York at night is both garish and subtle in its beauty.

107 *The promise of a bright billboard contrasts with the dark street and gray buildings around it.*

109 *A night view of Park Avenue. In the background the illuminated top of the Helmsley Building takes on a stately appearance.*

110/111 The night rain enhances the dazzling effect of the lights in Times Square.

112 People lingering at Lincoln Center are silhouetted by the bright fountain. The Center is the seat of the Metropolitan, the New York Philharmonic Orchestra and the New York City Ballet.

113 A detail of the inside of the Pan Am Building. The building has 58 floors and is octagonal in shape, with an interior geometric motif.

114/115 An evocative image of Times Square in the rain.

116 *Water tanks on the roofs of buildings are silhouetted by a glaring sun.*

PIER 3 GRANCOLOMBIANA

117 Lower Manhattan and the port seen
from the Brooklyn Promenade.

118/119 The awesome sight of a hurricane
approaching New York City.

120/121 The light of the sunset seems
to mellow the outlines of the skyscrapers,
which stand out on the horizon.